Spiritual influencer

a Journal for the Journey...

Copyright © 2020
Om Mys Murray LLC
All Rights Reserved
ISBN 978-1-7356106-0-3

Statement of Awareness

My name is

_____

_____

I Am a Spiritual Influencer.
I acknowledge that the spiritual and emotional energy of my thoughts, words, and actions emits a vibration that impacts and influences those around me.
What I demonstrate resonates.

Date of Opening Entry:

_____

_____

Date of Closing Entry:

_____

_____

Milestones

Page:
_____
_____
_____
_____

Page:
_____
_____
_____
_____

Page:
_____
_____
_____
_____

Page:
_____
_____
_____
_____

www.ingramcontent.com/pod-product-compliance
Lightning Source LLC
Chambersburg PA
CBHW031452040426
42444CB00007B/1070